Just Like Me Too!

Anne Rugari
Illustrated by
Gina Rugari

Copyright © 2020 by Anne Rugari. All rights reserved.

This book or any portion thereof may not be reproduced or used in any manner whatsoever without the express written permission of the publisher except for the use of brief quotations in a scholarly work or book review. For permissions or further information contact Braughler Books LLC at:

   info@braughlerbooks.com

Printed in the United States of America
Published by Braughler Books LLC., Springboro, Ohio

First printing, 2021

ISBN: 978-1-970063-37-0

Library of Congress Control Number: 2019916984

Ordering information: Special discounts are available on quantity purchases by bookstores, corporations, associations, and others. For details, contact the publisher at:

   sales@braughlerbooks.com
   or at 937-58-BOOKS

For questions or comments about this book, please write to:

   info@braughlerbooks.com

Braughler™ Books
braughlerbooks.com

"**Just Like Me Too!**" is a teaching tool for parents and teachers who want to help children understand and accept others. Children can be taught to recognize and celebrate everyone's unique differences! This book and my first book, "**Just Like Me!**" will help all children understand that boys and girls who don't look like them or act like them are just like them on the inside. All boys and girls have dreams, hopes, and goals with the only difference being how they accomplish them. Hopefully this book will help encourage inclusivity and understanding of all children who are differently-abled.

It's such an important life lesson!

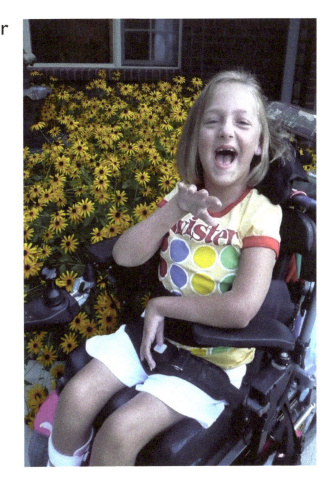

Both **Just Like Me!** books are about my daughter, Gina Rugari. Gina was diagnosed with Krabbe disease, a Leukodystrophy, as a newborn. Her journey to high school was filled with joy, laughter, tears, struggles, and so many accomplishments. Gina was a confident individual with a bubbly personality. She loved her crazy painted fingernails, swimming, traveling, and socializing with typical peers. She was a very active member of her community participating in Girl Scouting for ten years, and engaging in a variety of community service activities. She played soccer, wrote many of her own books, and was amazing on the computer. Gina was an excellent artist with a number of her original works displayed throughout this book. Even though she continued to lose muscle control and finger dexterity during her life, she became a wonderful teacher. Gina was a lesson in love, bravery, and persistence for so many classmates, teammates, friends and adults.

"No matter who we are, inside our hearts, we are more alike than we are different."

With love, compassion, and understanding,

Anne Rugari

SCHOOL SPIRIT

Gina is always excited about going to school. She has been on the Honor Roll for working hard and in third grade she was "Star of the Week!" Gina's friends describe her as, "courageous, helpful, friendly, kind, funny, responsible, wise, patient, obedient, and honest." Gina has an assistant at school that helps her with getting her school bag and supplies ready. Some students, like Gina, use computers to help them talk or write. She is very good with computers and even makes jokes on her computer. Do you know someone that uses equipment for Walking? Speaking? Hearing?

How would you describe your school spirit?

THE SCHOOL BUS

Riding the bus means you're pretty grown-up and it's a time to hang out with your friends. Gina was so excited on her first day of school when she got to ride the school bus! Some students need help to get on and off the bus. All schools have buses with special ramps for students in wheelchairs to be able to ride the bus. Gina is very independent and can drive her wheelchair on the ramp by herself. How do you get to school?

THE JOKER

Gina likes to play jokes on people and make them laugh. This is a picture Gina made in art class of her mother! In the picture, Gina's mom has a scrub brush and a toilet plunger in her hands. This made Gina's mom laugh because her mom isn't a plumber. Gina has a great sense of humor. She sometimes likes to play hide and seek in her wheelchair so no one can find her. She thinks it is funny to drive as fast as she can to run away from everyone in her wheelchair. When she's far ahead of them she will stop and turn around and laugh. Do you see all the stuffed animals hanging from Gina's chair? Gina likes decorating her wheelchair for special occasions and for fun. She knows that it will make people smile! Do you play jokes on people? What do you do to make people laugh and smile?

IMAGINATION

Gina has a great imagination! What do you see in this piece of art? Gina calls it Imagination Dragon. Do you see the dragon in the picture? Kids who have rare diseases may be differently-abled but have special talents and imaginations just like you do! What are your special talents? Gina enjoys expressing herself in talent shows. Here she is dressed up like Minnie Mouse and was performing a dance in her wheelchair. She has been a witch, a doctor, a mummy, a pirate, a ghost and Jessie from Toy Story, just to name a few. How do you like to express yourself? Where does your imagination take you?

MY FAVORITE THINGS

Gina has so much fun at the beach. She loves to make sand castles and sometimes even likes to be buried in the sand! Gina enjoys traveling to discover new places with her mom, but the beach is her favorite place to go. Have you ever seen the ocean or a big lake? Do you like to play in the sand? Sometimes when Gina goes to the beach she uses a special wheelchair that can go in the water. She really likes the waves splashing up on her. What is your favorite thing to do on vacation?

Gina loves her dog, Bella Rina. Gina named Bella and chose Rina as her middle name because it rhymes with Gina! Bella is a Maltese and only weighs about 10 pounds. Bella goes everywhere with Gina except to school. Bella is very devoted to Gina and even sleeps in bed with her at night. She is always waiting at the door for Gina to come home from school. Bella travels with Gina on her vacations. As you can see in this photo, Bella is wearing a life vest just like Gina to float in the water! Bella loves to swim and play at the beach too! Isn't she cute? Do you have a favorite pet that is your best friend?

STARRY NIGHT

Just like everyone else, Gina has school assignments. Gina enjoys her art classes and has many of her own unique pieces of art. Gina made this painting as part of an art assignment about Vincent Van Gogh, a famous artist. After the teacher taught the students about his art, Gina chose to create her own version of the artist's famous painting called "Starry Night." Gina is an artist and has her own creative style. Her creativity is also expressed in the way she dresses. How do you display your unique and creative style?

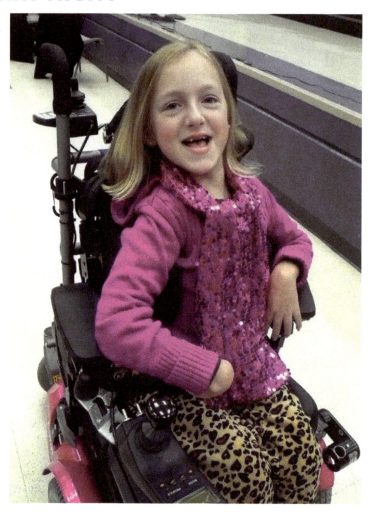

THE DANCE

Do you like music? Have you noticed how everyone dances differently to music? Gina LOVES music and LOVES to DANCE! Did you notice she's in a special chair? Gina dances in a wheelchair and can even do the limbo. Have you ever tried the limbo? Gina enjoys having dance parties with her friends. They play lots of music and everyone dances in their own unique way. Gina's wheelchair helps her to do all the things kids love to do. What is your favorite music? Do you have a favorite way to dance?

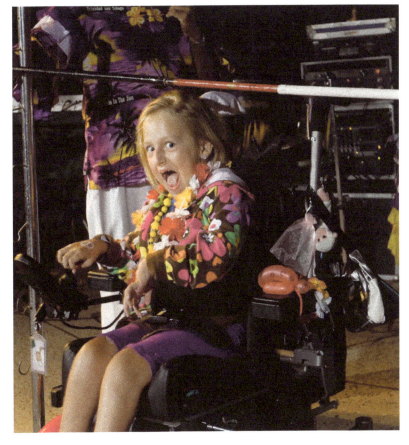

FIREWORKS

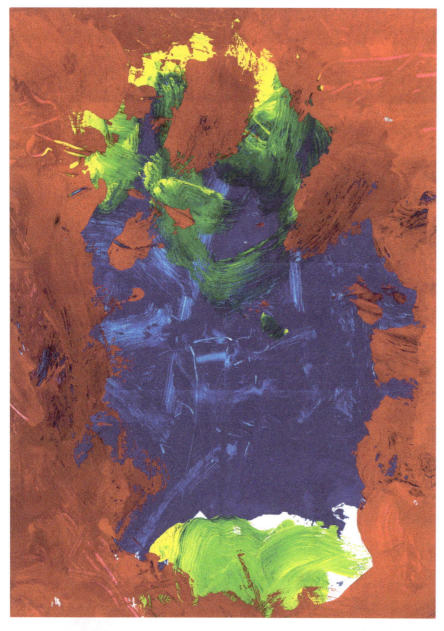

One of Gina's favorite holidays is the Fourth of July with all of fireworks! She is very patriotic and loves to celebrate by going to parades with lots of floats and people in them. It's so much fun to get up early and decorate her wheelchair for the parade with streamers and flags. Gina even decorates her fingernails to show her patriotic spirit. The city where Gina lives has lots of celebrations for different events, which always have big fireworks when it gets dark. Gina really enjoys the bright colors that light up the sky especially when they have a loud bang! Gina went to her first rock music concert on the Fourth of July and loved it! How do you celebrate special events?

THIS LITTLE LIGHT OF MINE

Gina is a Girl Scout and enjoys participating in everything her troop does. She knows the Girl Scout promise and wears her Girl Scout uniform to meetings and events. Her troop is made up of 26 girls, who all have fun on campouts and other activities. Gina knows all of the Girl Scout songs and her favorite is, "This Little Light of Mine." She is so proud of all the badges she earned as a Girl Scout. Clubs are fun to belong to because you can make lots of friends and learn new things. One year Gina sold 800 boxes of cookies! Her favorites are Thin Mints and Shortbread. What is your favorite Girl Scout cookie? Have you been part of a fun club or team?

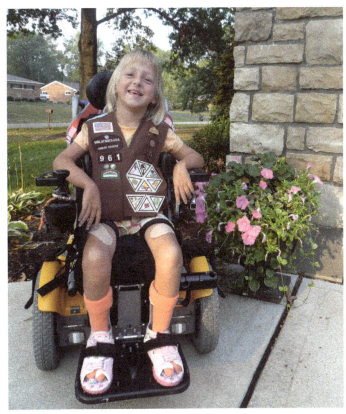

GREEN GRASS

Have you ever seen girls and boys play wheelchair soccer? The best part of wheelchair soccer is that they play with a special ball that is huge. The large ball makes it easier for the kids to kick from a wheelchair. In wheelchair soccer the rules are exactly the same as regular soccer. There's a team with defenders, forwards and even a goalkeeper! Teams that play well go to the state level of competition. Gina has won medals for soccer and even won a trophy for her best game!

Do you have a favorite sport that you play? Do you have a favorite team that you cheer for?

THE SLOPES

Even though Gina can't walk by herself, she can snow ski. The snow skis are adapted for boys and girls who can't stand by themselves. They are designed like a sled. There is an adaptive snow ski helper who rides on the back of the skis to help Gina stay on course. Gina rides the ski lift to the top of the slope just like everybody else does. Gina's artwork shows her favorite slope that she has skied down, a Black Diamond, the highest peak at a ski resort! Have you ever tried to snow ski?

FALL FUN

What is your favorite season? Gina enjoys the fall and created this piece of art using a variety of shapes to show falling leaves from a tree. The leaves are all colorful and different. Gina's favorite fall activities include camping, hiking in her wheelchair, playing in the leaves, and eating s'mores made over a campfire. Have you ever had s'mores? One time on a fall Girl Scout camping trip, Gina went rock climbing! She needs a little help to climb, but can go up the side of the rock just like you would. Have you ever been rock climbing? What is your favorite fall activity?

BELLA

In the fall, Bella goes with Gina to the pumpkin patch to pick out BIG pumpkins to carve. Did you know that Bella is a service dog? A service dog is trained to help a person with disabilities. Some service dogs help people who are blind. Some dogs are trained to detect seizures in people. Service dogs must be healthy, friendly, alert, perceptive, devoted, and loyal to the person they help. Bella is on duty here, watching over Gina. Service dogs take their job very seriously. Gina painted this picture of Bella and hung it in her room. Do you see Bella in the painting? Do you know anyone with a service dog?

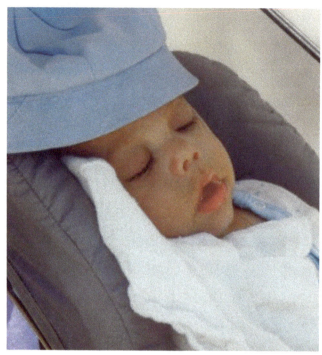

CIRCLE OF LOVE

All boys and girls want to feel safe, loved and special. Even though Gina and her brother, Nicholas, were born with a disease called Krabbe (crab-ay), many people love and care about them. It doesn't matter if a girl or boy looks or acts differently than other people, they still deserve kindness, compassion and acceptance for who they are. Everyone is DIFFERENT and UNIQUE which makes each of us special. There are many different (or diverse) people in the world. We may even learn something from each other's unique way of doing things. Gina's artwork displays that she wants everyone to be accepted and in the circle of love. How do you include people that are differently-abled or diverse?

HANDS

Gina cherishes all of her friends and just like her, they have different qualities and are unique in their own special way. She created this piece of art by tracing her own arms and hands and decorated each of them differently. That's the best thing about each of us is that there is only one of you. It doesn't matter how someone walks, looks, talks, dresses or does things differently, they can still be our friends. They can teach us something new. All boys and girls have feelings and are one-of-a-kind. Gina likes to say, they are: *"Just like me!"*

So often children who are differently-abled experience isolation and loneliness as a result of their condition. "Just Like Me!" is a wonderful and sensitively written teaching tool that allows children of any ability to learn about those who only appear different but in reality are "Just Like Me!" ~Patti, CEO of Engage Health

The message in "Just Like Me!" is so powerful and needed in our culture. It is important to understand that all of the special "differently-abled" children have a mind and heart just like other children. ~Jacque, Krabbe disease Advocate and Grandparent

"Just Like Me Too!" is a refreshing narrative that highlights the similarities between all students regardless of their abilities. I strongly feel that this book is a resource that should be in every classroom to support our students. ~Abbie, Special Education Teacher

"Just Like Me!" and "Just Like Me, Too!" are books that help students to set the standards on how to handle differences. As an observer of the interactions between Gina and her schoolmates, a valuable lesson was learned that kids care and can handle differences when they have had the opportunity to learn about diversity and inclusiveness. ~Charlie, School Board Member

"Just Like Me!" helps share the very important message that differences don't have to separate us. Some of us need different types of support to get through our day, but we all enjoy life's simple pleasures like friendship and laughter regardless of our needs. ~Brittney, Special Education Teacher

FACTS

- Krabbe disease, aka Globoid Cell Leukodystrophy is a rare, degenerative disorder
- Krabbe disease affects the Central and Peripheral Nervous Systems
- Affected patients are missing an enzyme that makes myelin, the coating around the nerves
- Babies born with the Early Infantile form typically die within the first few years of life
- The only treatment currently available is a cord blood or stem cell transplant
- Early diagnosis is imperative for treatment and only a few states screen for this disorder at birth
- 1 in 10 Americans has a rare disease
- 7000 Rare Diseases exist; less than 500 have FDA approved treatments
- 30 million people are affected by rare diseases and more than half are children
- 80% of rare diseases are genetically based

ABOUT THE AUTHOR

While raising her healthy first son, Philip, Anne Rugari lost a second son, Nick, to Krabbe disease in 1987. He was only a year old when he passed away. Anne knew as she was expecting her third child in 1999, that the baby should be tested at birth for Krabbe disease. Gina tested positive and received an umbilical cord blood transplant at just three weeks of age to give her the missing enzyme she needed to stabilize the disease. Gina Rugari was a pioneer in the Krabbe world of medicine and research, being the fourth newborn in the world to receive a treatment for this terminal disease. During her lifetime, she couldn't walk and used a computer to talk. Gina was cognitively age appropriate throughout her life. She attended school through her freshman year of high school. As her disease progressed to her peripheral nervous system, Gina lost her battle with Krabbe in the summer of 2015.

From Anne's experiences with Krabbe disease and the loss of two of her three children, she was inspired to create awareness and educational opportunities to support patients and families affected by Krabbe. Anne founded Partners For Krabbe Research (P4KR) to support and advance research by funding and collaborating with scientists, researchers and clinicians. Anne also is the Co-Founder and Vice-President of KrabbeConnect, a non-profit that bridges the gap between science and patient knowledge. **Just Like Me Too!** is the second of two children's books that Anne has written and published. Anne is dedicated to changing the outcomes of those affected by this terminal disease. She hopes that there will be an effective treatment and possible cure for patients diagnosed with Krabbe disease.

As a volunteer, Anne continues to expand her advocacy role in the rare disease community. She works tirelessly to ensure that the needs of those affected by other rare disorders receive the best care and treatment available. In her leisure time, Anne enjoys boating, walking the beach, riding her bike and making memories with her grandson, PJ.

CPSIA information can be obtained
at www.ICGtesting.com
Printed in the USA
BVHW020504220721
612495BV00002B/7